D1563978

# SAFETY
# ZONE

## A Book Teaching Children
## Abduction Prevention Skills

by

Linda D. Meyer

Foreword by
John and Revé Walsh

Illustrations by
Marina Megale

*The Chas. Franklin Press*
*18409-90th Avenue W., Edmonds, WA 98020*

Text copyright © 1984 by Linda D. Meyer. Illustrations copyright © 1984 by Marina Megale. All rights reserved. This book, or parts thereof, may not be used or reproduced in any way, shape or form except for brief excerpts for review without the written permission of the publisher. ISBN 0-9603516-7-1 (soft), ISBN 0-9603516-8-x (lib. bind.) Library of Congress Catalogue Card Number: 84-080039. Printed in the United States of America.

# ACKNOWLEDGEMENTS

Many people have been involved with the development of Safety Zone. In particular, I would like to thank MaryAnn and Bruce Prout, Peggy Meyer, Jacquie Ackley, Melodee McWilliams, Trudy Dana, Randy O'Connor, Linda Arnold and the Edmonds Writing school. Also, Kara and Heather Twenter, Shari, Debbie and Roberta Wennik, and Joshua, Matthew and Lee Meyer.

Last, but certainly not least, I wish to thank Sharon McMorris of the Adam Walsh Child Resource Center for her much appreciated support, and John and Revé Walsh, whose personal tragedy and perseverance has forced a sleeping nation to take notice of our national tragedy. While the idea was already brewing in my mind, it was the television portrayal "Adam," based on their true story, which was the catalyst for the writing of this book.

## THE CHILDREN'S SAFETY SERIES

PRIVATE ZONE: A Book Teaching Children Sexual Assault Prevention Tools

SAFETY ZONE: A Book Teaching Child Abduction Prevention Skills

HELP YOURSELF TO SAFETY: A Guide to Avoiding Dangerous Situations with Strangers and Friends

IT'S NOT YOUR FAULT

"A child prepared to respond to unwelcome advances and invitations is the child who will make wiser decisions when faced with possible danger. We teach water, traffic and bicycle safety to protect our children from harm. We cannot risk the consequences of neglecting to teach personal safety. SAFETY ZONE accomplishes this admirably."

Peggy Anderson, R.N.
School Nurse
Edmonds, WA

# DEDICATION
To all the Adam Walshes

# FOREWORD
by
John and Revé Walsh

Do we love our children? People respond to that question with amazement, "Of course we do, doesn't everyone?" Not everyone loves children. In 1982 there were over two million reported missing children and over 2.4 million reported cases of child abuse and sexual assault. No one has factual statistics as to what happened to those children, but at least 6,000 were murdered.

Our son was the victim of the ultimate form of child abuse — abduction and murder. And we continue in his memory, because we realize he was the real victim, as all children are potential victims. They are the silent, helpless, majority with no power, vote, platform or money to provide for their needs. It is up to us, the adults, to provide not only for their needs, but also for their safety. They are this country's greatest resource and its future. They look to us now for direction as we will look to them when they will determine our future.

This is 1984, and the belief that it can't happen to your child is as naive as was the assumption that the world was flat.

We believe that all children are everyone's responsibility. Show your love for your child and other children by reading this book and giving it to others. Give your children their chance at the future.

John and Revé Walsh
Adam Walsh Child Resource Center
Fort Lauderdale, Florida
February 1984

# Adult's Page

Child abduction with all its frightening implications is a subject which concerns even the most stalwart parent. A missing child conjures up multiple fears: Has he run away? Is he lost? Has he been kidnapped? Is he frightened? hurt? cold? hungry? And worse, has he been sexually assaulted, or is he even still alive?

The missing child is not a rare phenomenon. Each year over 1.8 million children are reported missing. About 90% run away of their own volition and return home a few days later. But many others are the involuntary victims of kidnapping. About 100,000 are abducted in parental custody fights, while for 50,000 there is no clue. They simply disappear.

There is increasing awareness of the creeping tide of this problem. Schools are undertaking safety programs, and parents are trying to teach their children wariness without teaching them fear. But what do you say? Where do you begin?

That is what this book is all about. Its purpose is multiple: 1) to teach children preventive measures through the use of a "read-aloud" section of hypothetical situations; 2) to show adults ways in which they can teach young ones caution; 3) to teach children to recognize dangerous or suspicious situations; 4) to teach problem-solving skills; and 5) to create an atmosphere of open discussion of a serious subject.

Safety is not a topic which can be discussed once and never mentioned again. Children forget! This book and these suggestions should be read and used at frequent intervals. Once is NOT enough!

Unfortunately, the abduction of children is a reality that won't automatically go away. Purposeful education gives children information they need to recognize and handle threatening situations. "Although there are no guarantees, **INFORMED CHILDREN ARE SAFER CHILDREN.**"*

* Frances S. Dayee, PRIVATE ZONE: A Book Teaching Children Sexual Assault Prevention Tools, Warner Books, 1984.

# SAFETY ZONE

This is Matt!

It's a pretty day outside, and he is walki
over to his friend's house to play. Dogs are
barking, birds are singing, and he is feeling
happy.

When he reaches the corner, Matt stops
and looks both ways to see if it's safe to cros
the street. A car drives up and stops in front
him.

"Hey, little boy," the man says. "I am
looking for my dog and I would sure like yo
help looking for him. If you'll help me find
him, you can have this candy."

Matt looks carefully at the man. Matt ha
this funny feeling that something isn't right. I
stands up tall and very firmly says "No, I
won't."

2

The man slides across the seat toward him and starts to reach for him.

But Matt is too smart for the man. Do you know what Matt does? Quick as a wink, he turns and runs lickety-split to his friend's house. Straight to safety!

Did Matt do the right thing?

You bet he did! He did exactly the right thing. He said "No!" and ran, and his Mom would be very proud of him.

Now let's look at some other situations. And let's see how you should handle them.

Let's say you are playing with some friends in your front yard when a pretty lady drives up in a big beautiful car.

"Hello, little girl," she says with a big smile. "Come see what I have here in the car. I'll give you some candy."

5

What would you do?

She's smiling real pretty, and she looks like
nice lady. Would you go to the car and get
with her?

(Turn page for answer.)

6

No! You shouldn't. Do not even get near the car!

What **SHOULD** you do then?

That's right. You would yell **"NO!"** and run into the house to your Mom or Dad or babysitter. If no one is home, run to a neighbor's house. Ask your Mom or Dad who you should go to in an emergency.

You should never, ever go with **ANY**one- even if they offer you candy or cookies.

Good! Now you're getting the hang of it!

Now let's look at another one. This one's hard.

Your Mom and Dad don't live together, and you hardly ever see your Dad because yo live with your Mom. One day you're in a sto when your Dad comes up and says, "Jenny, come with me now. Your mother doesn't war you anymore. She said you're to come live with me now." Then he reaches out and grab your arm.

What would you do?

You would probably think, "Mom doesn' want me anymore? Oh, that makes me feel sad!"

But that is not the truth! Your Mom love you very, very much. And she would never, **EVER** give you away to anybody.

So what would you do?

You should yell real loud, "No!" Go ahead
and yell. It's okay. And run to the clerk and
say, "Please help me. That man is trying to
take me away from my Mom, and I'm not
supposed to live with him!"*

10

Now, this one is a real toughie. Tell me what you would do here:

You're getting out of school and a man drives up in a truck and says, "Hey, honey, come here with me. Your Mom is very sick, and she sent me to come get you. Get into the truck, and I'll take you to her."

What would you do? Do you believe him

No, don't believe him. He may be trying to trick you.

Okay, here we go again. What would you do?

Yell, "No!" Now turn around and run lickety-split!

Where would you run to? Did school just get out? Are you still out in front of it? Then run back to the school office. There you can tell the principal or secretary your problem, and they will take care of you.

What a good job you're doing!

Now, this is the hardest one you've had yet. Let's pretend that someone picks you up i his arms and puts you into his car and drives away with you. What would you do then?

First of all, **DON'T** buckle your seat belt. You want to be free to move fast. Next, remember a car isn't always moving. He will have to stop it sometime. Whether it's at a gas station, a grocery store, or just a stop light,

**JUMP OUT** and **RUN!** Wherever he stops the car, get out and run as fast as you can to the closest adult who will help you. What else might you do?

　　**YELL. RUN** real fast and **YELL!** It's okay. Ask your Mom or Dad or teacher if there is any other way they would like you to handle this situation.\*\*

What have we learned?

We have learned not to get into the car with anybody unless our parents tell us we can. We have learned how to yell "No!" We have learned to turn and run lickety-split! We have even learned how to get out of a car if we have to. Good show!

Now I want you to learn one more thing, and that is where to go for help. Where would you go for help? Who would you go to for help?

We've talked about a few of them already.

15

They were your mother, your principal or school secretary, your friend's mother, and the store clerk.

Who else might you go to for help? Can you guess?

It would probably also be safe to go to your father, your grandma or grandpa, your aunt or uncle, a police or fire officer, your teacher, your minister, an older brother, sister or cousin, or a woman with children. Go wherever you have to until you get help. Ask your Mom or Dad who it's safe to go to.

16

Boy, you've learned a lot! Remember this: Yell and run! **YOU DON'T ALWAYS HAVE TO BE POLITE TO A BIG PERSON. YOUR SAFETY IS MORE IMPORTANT.**

Wherever you are, whatever you are doing, you should never, ever—no matter wha they say—go with anyone unless your Mom o Dad tells you it's okay.

Every kid in the whole world has the righ to say "No!" and to run.

Especially you!

*Change the parent appropriately if the father has custody
**There are too many variables to handle in this short spac
Further discussion may be necessary which takes into account th
child's age, where the abduction takes place, where they go, and
whether people are around.

17

18

# TEACHING ABDUCTION PREVENTION SKILLS

There may be nothing more heartwrenching than to have one's child disappear. It taps the most basic of feelings: Love, fear, the need to shield one's young. But there is much we can do to protect our most precious natural resource. We needn't sit back and wring our hands, convinced that we are helpless. We are not. In this section we will explore ways in which we can help our children develop problem-solving skills to protect themselves.

First let us take a look at the way we raise our young. Perhaps you are like most of us. We want to rear children that are mature and intelligent, children that obey, children that are respectful of adults, that do what big people say. That is usually considered the ideal of the well brought up child.

Teaching children to be respectful and obey adults, however, may create a problem. Why? Because, while this practice assumes all adults are kind and caring of children, such is not the case! Some adults hurt children, and some adults will take advantage of a child's trust and respect to hurt him. **BY TEACHING OUR CHILDREN TO ALWAYS RESPECT, TRUST, AND OBEY ADULTS, WE ARE INADVERTENTLY SETTING THEM UP FOR ABDUCTION AND/OR ASSAULT.**

Since that is not what we really want to accomplish, then, we need to change what we teach our kids. We need to show them that there are also times and situations when we WANT them to question authority, when we WANT them to disobey big people. We need to teach them common sense and problem-solving skills.

# "WHAT IF...?"

"What if...?" is a game you can use to teach your child problem-solving. In the children's "read-aloud" section of this book, you read a number of hypothetical situations. These are examples of "what if...?" situations. In our family we use it when we want to teach our children some vital information in a fun way. We do it while driving or while at dinner. Anywhere is fine. In this way we have taught our children sexual assault prevention, abduction prevention, and basic first aid. Its applications are limitless, and we highly recommend the technique.

Here are some examples of "What if...?" situations you can use with your children:

"Joshua, what if you were walking at the beach, and a teen-ager comes up and says he found a seal, and he wants you to go with him to see it? What would you do?"

"Kelly, what if you and Sharlyn are walking to the store, and a man drives up and says he has lost his little boy, and would like you to please help find him? What would you do?"

"Adam, what if you're walking over to Jason's house, and a man in a uniform drives up and says, 'Son, your Dad was in an accident, and he told me to come get you?' What would you do?"

The possibilities are limitless. Use your imagination.

# ROLE-PLAYING

Role-playing is another fun way to teach children how you want them to handle situations. It is often easier to perform a given behavior if you have practiced it before. A child may be reluctant to yell and run in church unless he has practiced yelling and running and been given permission to do so anywhere and any time it is necessary. Here is where role-playing comes in handy: It programs children to behave in a certain way by giving them the opportunity to practice a given behavior. Role-playing is often combined with "What if...?", except that you act out the situation instead of only discussing it.

Let's use situation two above for an example. Say to your child: "Okay, Kelly and Sharlyn, let's say you're walking to the store, and a man drives up in a car and asks you to get in and come help him look for his lost little girl. Now you pretend to be the man, and I'll pretend to be the little girls. Okay?"

Then you act it out. Kelly and Sharlyn pretend to drive up in a car and ask you to get in. Then you show them what you want them to do. You yell "No, I won't," then turn around and run!

You have shown them exactly how you want them to handle this situation. Now reverse the roles to give them an opportunity to practice. You pretend to drive up in the car, and have them yell "No, I won't" and run.

Use this same method on as many situations as you can think of, and do it often. Once is not enough! Children forget!

# OTHER CONSIDERATIONS

* Teach your child his phone number including area code. Teach him to call collect and/or to dial 911. **ROLE-PLAY IT.**

* Put a metal bracelet on him which includes his name, address and phone number including area code. This may not be useful in the event of an abduction, but will help if the child becomes lost.

* Write your phone number including area code inside the tags of all his shirts or her blouses. In this way his name will always be with him even if he should forget the number itself.

* Be aware that the most dangerous places for potential abductions are carnivals, fairs, shopping malls, and public restrooms.

* Do not leave children out of view and unsupervised in public parks, malls, etc.

* Accompany children to bathrooms in public places.

* Make sure your child's day care facility or school will not release him to **ANYBODY** but you without your permission.

* Tell him he is **NEVER** to go with your divorced spouse unless you have told the child ahead of time of the arrangement.

* Tell him if a divorced spouse does keep him longer than he understood he would be with him, to call you from anywhere as soon as possible.

* Always know where your child is going to play. When he gets to his friend's house, instruct him to call you to let you know he has arrived safely.

* We cannot always be with our children, and the time comes when we must allow them the freedom to grow and to become independent. As you send your child off into a situation which you would have supervised in the past, say: 1) "Now what are the rules?"

and have him give you the basics, then as he gets older: 2) "Remember the rules."

* Instruct your child to kick and scream if anyone ever grabs his arm or tries to pick him up and carry him. **ROLE-PLAY IT.**

* Warn your child not to ever let anyone know that he or she is alone in the house. Give him permission to lie if necessary. When he answers the phone, he can say, "My Mom can't come to the phone right now. Can I take a message?"

* Tell your child where he should go for help if you are not home. Clear it ahead of time with the person you want him to go to.

* Do **NOT** say when you are going out for the evening, "Now, you be sure to mind the babysitter!" This is a common example of inadvertently setting our children up for a dangerous situation, e.g. sexual assault. (See PRIVATE ZONE: A Book Teaching Children Sexual Assault Prevention Tools by Frances S. Dayee to teach sexual assault prevention.)

* Abductors will often try to enlist the aid or sympathy of the child. Tell your children that as much as you appreciate their compassion, they should **NEVER** go with anybody, but should come ask you for help.

* Teach your children the "buddy system." There is strength and more safety in numbers.

* Do not allow your children to wear T-shirts or clothing of any sort with their names on it. A stranger may be able to convince a child they know one another by using the child's name, thus facilitating an abduction.

* Tell your child who among your friends and relatives he or she may accept a ride from or go to for safety. Not even friends and relatives may be safe!

Eighty-five percent of child sexual assaults are perpetrated by someone the child knows!

&ast; Arrange a password with your child. Before they will accept a ride with **ANYONE**, the person must give them the agreed upon password. Tell your child not to let **ANYBODY** know what the password is.

&ast; Tell your child never to accept a ride home from school with anybody unless 1) you call the school to have the school tell them it's okay, or 2) the person gives the password.

&ast; Give your child permission to say "No" to an adult.

&ast; Walk your child's school route with him, checking for hazards. Avoid vacant lots and fields with bushes as well as alleys which are not well-traveled.

# ABDUCTION PROOFING YOUR COMMUNITY

\* Organize an absentee calling committee at your local school. Someone from the committee will go to the school daily to call the homes or parental work places of those children who do not arrive to be sure that they are home sick and have not gotten lost on the way to school.

\* (I had originally intended to suggest that you make your area a Block Parent Protected Area. Police departments are concerned about this program now, however, because bogus signs are showing up to lure children to unsafe homes. Be wary.)

\* Be watchful. Report anything unusual to the police. If you see something suspect taking place with a child, **DO NOT BE AFRAID TO BECOME INVOLVED. AN ABDUCTION MAY BE TAKING PLACE.**

\* Lobby for a child safety program in your local schools. It might include instruction in sexual assault, abduction, and drug abuse prevention, basic safety and first aid, and what to do in case of an emergency. Offer a parent's night with a guest speaker and a book store offering books on these subjects. **AN INFORMED COMMUNITY IS A SAFER COMMUNITY.**

\* Have your children finger-printed. Keep copies in your safe deposit boxes, in your children's baby books, and perhaps at relatives' houses. Also include a recent photograph, blood type and lock of hair. These would be useful for identification in the event of an abduction. Be sure your dentist has dental records.

\* Meet with mall and store managers to arrange that store doors would be immediately closed and locked if a child is reported missing. Shoppers' inconvenience is a small price to pay for the safety of a child.

We needn't sit back in impotence. There is much we can do to make our children safer.

# WHAT TO DO IF YOUR CHILD IS MISSING?

1. **STAY CALM.** It is so easy to lose one's head in this situation. But you mustn't. It is mandatory that you remain calm so you can think.

2. Call where you think he **SHOULD** be.

3. Call where you think he **MIGHT** be.

4. Call your spouse.

5. Call the police. If the child is not found promptly, be sure they file a missing child report with the FBI. If they refuse to, **DO SO YOURSELF**. (This was made possible by the passage of the Missing Children's Act of the United States on September 30, 1982.)

6. Do not be surprised if the police investigate parents, friends, and relatives. It is common procedure, and no one is above suspicion.

7. Call any friends or relatives who you think might be able to help.

8. Organize a search party.

9. Call one of the organizations listed below. They know what you're going through and may be able to help.

10. Call Child Find and the Missing Children Help Center to have your child listed in a central computer for tracking. (See numbers under Resources: Organizations.)

11. Put up posters around the community.

12. Eventually, if needed, join a support group.

13. Advertise in out-of-town newspapers, especially if you think an ex-spouse may have abducted the child.

WESTPORT FREE PUBLIC LIBRARY
408 OLD COUNTY ROAD
WESTPORT, MASSACHUSETTS 02790

## RESOURCES: ORGANIZATIONS

These first four organizations will be useful resources in the case of an abduction.

Adam Walsh Child Resource Center
1876 N. University Drive #306
Fort Lauderdale, FL 33322
Ph. (305) 475-4847

Child Find
P.O. Box 277
New Paltz, NY 12561
Ph. 1-800-431-5005

Child Find of Canada
Box G145, Station G
Calgary, Alberta T3B 3B7
Ph. (403) 288-3344

Child Search
6 Beacon Street
Boston, MA 02108
Ph. (617) 720-1760

Missing Children...Help Center
410 Ware Blvd. #1102
Tampa, FL 33619
Ph. (813) 681-HELP or 623-KIDS

National Center for Missing
  and Exploited Children
1835 K Street N.W., #700
Washington, D.C. 20006
Ph. (202) 634-9821

The following organization gives workshops teaching parents child personal safety:

Safety and Fitness Effort (SAFE)
541 Avenue of the Americas
New York, NY 10011
Ph. (212) 242-4874

# RESOURCES: BOOKS

Unfortunately I have not been able to locate any books that teach children abduction prevention. The following resources are generally the stories of adults or children who have been kidnapped.

Hostage: A Police Approach To A Contemporary Crisis; Maher, George F.; 1977, C.C. Thomas.

Kidnapped At Chowchilla; Miller, Gail and Tompkins, Sandra; 1977, Logos.

Kidnap: The Story of the Lindbergh Case; Waller, George; 1961, Dial Press.

Somewhere Child; Black, Bonnie Lee; 1981, Viking Press. (Fiction)

Stolen Children: How and Why Parents Kidnap Their Kids — And What To Do About It; Gill, John Edward; 1981, Seaview Books.

Why Have They Taken Our Children?; Baugh, Jack and Morgan, Jefferson; 1979, Dell. (The Chowchilla Case)

## Author's Biography

Linda Meyer is a native of Santa Barbara, California and makes her home with her husband and two young sons in the State of Washington. She has a B.A. from San Jose State University in social psychology.

She also has written THE CESAREAN (R)EVOLUTION: A Handbook for Parents and Professionals and co-authored RESPONSIBLE CHILDBIRTH: How To Give Birth Normally and Avoid a Caesarean Section, and has edited and published HELP FOR DEPRESSED MOTHERS, PRIVATE ZONE: A Book Teaching Children Sexual Assault Prevention Tools, and SPECIAL DELIVERY: A Book for Kids About Cesarean and Vaginal Birth. She is currently working on two novels.

## Illustrator's Biography

Marina Megale is a native and resident of Seattle. She is a graduate of Cornish Institute of Allied Arts.

She is a free lance artist with a number of books to her credit including: PRIVATE ZONE: A Book Teaching Children Sexual Assault Prevention Tools and the Children's Problem Solving Series: I WANT IT, I CAN'T WAIT, I WANT TO PLAY, and MY NAME'S NOT DUMMY, and KIDS CAN COOPERATE, all by Elizabeth Crary.